SECOND EDITION

American Start with English

Student Book 4

D. H. Howe

OXFORD UNIVERSITY PRESS

Oxford University Press

198 Madison Avenue
New York, NY 10016 USA

Great Clarendon Street
Oxford OX2 6DP England

Oxford   New York
Athens   Auckland   Bangkok   Bogota   Bombay
Buenos Aires   Calcutta   Cape Town   Dar es Salaam
Delhi   Florence   Hong Kong   Istanbul   Karachi
Kuala Lumpur   Madras   Madrid   Melbourne
Mexico City   Nairobi   Paris   Singapore
Taipei   Tokyo   Toronto   Warsaw

and associated companies in
Berlin   Ibadan

OXFORD is a trademark of Oxford University Press

ISBN 0-19-434025-2

Copyright © 1996 Oxford University Press

EDITORIAL MANAGER: Shelagh Speers
EDITOR: Edward Yoshioka
ASSISTANT EDITOR: Lynne Robertson
PRODUCTION AND DESIGN: OUP International Education Unit
and Oxprint Design
ASSOCIATE PRODUCTION EDITOR: Joseph McGasko
PRODUCTION COORDINATOR: Ahmad Sadiq
PRODUCTION MANAGER: Abram Hall

COVER DESIGN: April Okano
COVER PHOTOGRAPH: Alan Kaplan

ILLUSTRATIONS: Val Biro

Printing (last digit): 10 9 8 7 6 5 4 3

Printed in Hong Kong

Contents

American
Start with English

Review

1. *Point and say around the class.*

A: No. 1 is a ball but No. 2 is not a ball.
              It is a drum.
B: No. 2 is a drum but No. 3 is not a drum.
              It is a tree.

1. a ball	2. a drum	3. a tree	4. a horse	5. a plane	6. a purse	7. a firefighter
8. a glass	9. a hammer	10. a nail	11. a needle	12. a pin	13. a truck	14. a package
15. a bowl	16. a doctor	17. a laborer	18. a queen	19. a bandage	20. a skirt	21. a wrist
22. an ankle	23. a shoulder	24. a chain	25. a square	26. a flag	27. a ship	28. a stamp
29. an envelope	30. a circle	31. a blanket	32. a cracker	33. a bucket	34. a collar	35. a jug

2. *Point, ask, and answer.*

A: Look at a. Who has a red shirt?
B: John has a red shirt and Peter has one, too.
A: Look at b. Who has some flowers?
B: Mrs. Bell has some flowers and Mary has some, too.

John	Peter	Mrs. Bell	Mary	The man	the boy
a.		b.		c.	
a red shirt		some flowers		some cans	

The soldier	the sailor	The boy	the girl	The man	the boy
d.		e.		f.	
a hat		a kitten		a kite	

John	Mary	John	the dog	The doctor	the nurse
g.		h.		i.	
some flags		a coat		a bandage	

3. *Add* me, you, him, it, us, *or* them.

a. "Please listen to _____ . I am talking to ____ ."
b. "Can you see Mary and Peter?" "I can see ____ but I cannot see ____ ."
c. "I have red socks. Can you see _____ ?"
d. "We are behind this big tree. They cannot see ____ but we can see _____ ."
e. "That is not a dog. Look at ____ ! It is a cat!"
f. "Can you see the men?" "No. You are standing in front of ____ . I cannot see _____ ."

Review

4. *Point, ask, and answer.*

A: Are there any men in the boat? Are there any women?
B: There are some men in the boat but there aren't any women.
A: Is there any milk in the glass? Is there any ink?
B: There is some milk in the glass but there isn't any ink.

men?	milk?	socks?	coffee?	stockings?	a can?	fruit?
a.	b.	c.	d.	e.	f.	g.
women?	ink?	shoes?	rice?	socks?	a box?	milk?

clocks?	ice?	sand?	scissors?	meat?	cups?	paint?
h.	i.	j.	k.	l.	m.	n.
books?	coffee?	water?	knives?	bread?	plates?	tea?

5. *Point, ask, and answer.*

A: How is he going to school?
B: He is going to school by bus.

to school	to work	to school	to work	to school	to work
a.	b.	c.	d.	e.	f.
by bus	by car	by bicycle	by train	on foot	by boat

6. *Answer:* Yes, I can, *or* No, I can't.

a. Can you read?
b. Can you write?
c. Can you fly?

d. Can you touch the ceiling?
e. Can you write with a ruler?
f. Can you write with a pencil?

3

Review

7. *Make sentences like these.*

A: The boy is taller than the girl.
B: The girl is shorter than the boy.

taller	longer	bigger	stronger	older	faster	cleaner
a.	b.	c.	d.	e.	f.	g.
shorter	shorter	smaller	weaker	younger	slower	dirtier

8. *Give the missing words.*

a. happy – happier
b. easy –
c. heavy –
d. hungry –
e. ugly –
f. thick –
g. thin –

h. beautiful – more beautiful
i. dangerous –
j. careful –
k. careless –
l. clever –
m. good –
n. bad –

9. *Choose the right answer.*

a. The children put down (their, our, his) pens and listened to the teacher.
b. That kitten cannot see (its, their, her) mother.
c. We wrote (our, your, their) names on the first page of the book.
d. The dogs had black feet but (its, their, her) ears were white.
e. The kitten was black but (his, their, its) tail was white.
f. "Hold up (their, there, your) books," the teacher said to the class.
g. The children took off (his, her, their) coats because it was hot.

10. *Add* someone, anyone, something, *or* anything.

a. I can hear someone but I can't see . . . Can you see . . . ?
b. Is there anything under the desk? No, there isn't . . . under the desk but there is . . . under the chair.

11. *Point and say.*

A: Mr. Jones is a laborer.
B: Mr. Hall is a doctor.

a laborer	a doctor	a nurse	a soldier	a police officer	a fisherman
a.	b.	c.	d.	e.	f.
Mr. Jones	Mr. Hall	Miss Rose	Andy Brown	This woman	Mr. Rose

a sailor	a gardener	a storekeeper	a teacher	a farmer
g.	h.	i.	j.	k.
John Bell	Mr. White	Mr. Lee	Susan	Mr. Long

12. *Make up sentences like these.*

A: May I have a pen, please?   B. Yes. Here it is!
A: May I have some books, please?   B. Yes. Here they are!

13. *Point, ask, and answer.*

A: What time is it?
B: It's twelve o'clock.

5

14. *Choose the right words.*

   a. Yesterday (is, was, are, were) a holiday. Today (is, was, are, were) not a holiday.

   b. Today May (has, have, had) an apple. Yesterday she (has, have, had) an orange.

   c. Today the children (is, was, are, were) in the classroom. Yesterday they (is, was, are, were) not in the classroom.

   d. Today I (has, have, had) breakfast at half past seven. I (has, have, had) it at half past seven every day.

   e. Last year we (has, have, had) forty desks in our classroom. This year we (has, have, had) forty-five desks.

15. *Change these sentences into questions and give short answers.*

   Examples: Today is a holiday. Is today a holiday? Yes, it is.
   Yesterday was not a holiday. Was yesterday a holiday?
   No, it wasn't.

   a. Yesterday was a holiday.   g. This is our classroom.
   b. Today is not a holiday.   h. That is not our classroom.
   c. Today is hot.   i. We are working.
   d. Yesterday was not hot.   j. We are not sleeping.
   e. Today is not Sunday.   k. They were at school yesterday.
   f. Yesterday was not Saturday.   l. They were not at home yesterday.

16. *Add* my, your, his, her, its, our, *or* their.

   a. "Peter, please hold up _____ book."
      "Yes, Miss Hall. I am holding up _____ book."
      "Is he holding up _____ book?" "Yes, he is."
   b. "Mary, please hold up _____ book."
      "Yes, Miss Hall. I am holding up _____ book."
      "Is she holding up _____ book?" "Yes, she is."
   c. "Boys and girls, hold up _____ books, please."
      "Yes, Miss Hall. We are holding up _____ books."
      "Are they holding up _____ books?" "Yes, they are."
   d. "Look at that dog. _____ front legs are shorter than _____ back legs!"

1. *Read.*

a.

2. *Read.*

This is Betty. This is Peter.

  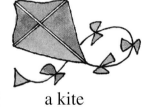 

a purse a drawing a kite a ball

an envelope a ring a boat a map

These are Betty's things.
They are hers.

These are Peter's things.
They are his.

3. *Finish these sentences about Betty and Peter.*

The purse is hers.
The ball is his.
The drawing is . . .
The map is . . .
The envelope is . . .
The kite is . . .
The ring is . . .
The boat is . . .

4. *Read.*

a.

5. *Practice this rhyme.*

A: My shirt is dirty but yours is clean.
B: My ball is yellow but yours is green.

A: My face is happy but yours is sad.
B: My marks are good but yours are bad.

6. *Put in* mine, yours, hers, his, ours, *or* theirs.

a. This is my pencil. It is _____ .

b. This is your pencil. It is _____ .

c. These are our rulers. They are _____ .

d. Those are his shoes. They are _____ .

e. Those are her shoes. They are _____ .

f. This is our playground. It is _____ .

g. That is the girls' playground. It is _____ .

h. That is the boys' playground. It is _____ .

1. *Read and then finish the sentences.*

This is the Lee family.
It is eight o'clock.
They are having a meal.
They are having dinner.
They are having rice and fish
for dinner.

a. I am not . . . dinner now.
b. I am . . . having breakfast now.
c. I . . . lunch now.
d. I am having an . . . lesson now.
e. I am not having a . . . lesson.
f. I am not . . . lesson.

2. *Read.*

A: What is this girl doing?
B: She is taking a bath.

3. *Read.*

1.

   The boys are having a snack.

2.

   The girls are having a drink.

3.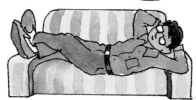

   Mr. Lee is taking a nap.

4.

   Peter is taking a bath.

5.

   Mary is taking a ride.

6.

   Mrs. Lee is taking a walk.

7.

   The children are having a party.

8.

   John is taking a ride.

4. *Ask and answer questions like these about the people on page 12.*

A: What are the boys doing?
B: They are having a snack.

A: What is Peter doing?
B: He is taking a bath.

5. *Read and answer the questions.*

This is Peter.

He is not at school.

He is in bed.

He is sick.

He has a cold.

a. Are you at school?

b. Are you in bed?

c. Are you sick?

d. Do you have a cold?

e. Does your father have a cold?

f. Does your mother have a cold?

g. Does your friend have a cold?

6. Review. *Give short answers to the questions.*

a. Is this your kite? Yes, it is mine.
b. Are these my clothes? Yes, they are yours.
c. Is this my purse? Yes, it is . . .
d. Is this your ring? Yes, . . .
e. Is this Peter's map? Yes . . .
f. Is this Betty's drawing?
g. Is this our classroom?
h. Are these your chairs?
i. Is that their classroom?

7. *Put in* taller, bigger, more beautiful, better, *or* worse.

a. My brother is tall but yours is . . . than mine.
b. Our classroom is big but theirs is . . . than ours.
c. Her drawing was beautiful but his was . . . than hers.
d. His marks were good but hers were . . . than his.
e. My writing is bad but yours is . . . than mine.

8. *Read aloud.*

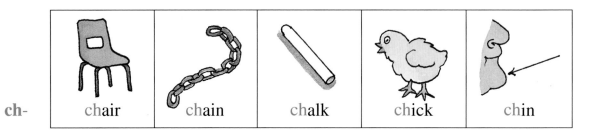

ch-   chair   chain   chalk   chick   chin

cheap   children

-ch   switch   matches   teacher   lunch

14

1. *What did they do?*

    a. John looked in the window.
    b. He knocked on the door.
    c. Mary opened the door.
    d. John walked into the classroom.
    e. Mary closed the door.
    f. The teacher pointed to the board.
    g. John cleaned the board.
    h. The teacher smiled.
       She thanked John. She said, "Thank you, John!"
    i. John walked back to his place.

Now ask questions.
A: Did John look in the window?
B: Yes, he did. He looked in the window.

2. *Read.*

Yesterday

a. Mary went to school by bus.
John went to school by car.
Peter went to school on foot.

b. Mary wore a yellow dress.
John wore a green shirt.
Peter wore blue pants.

c. They all got to school at eight-thirty.

d. Mary sat in the front of the class.
John sat in the middle of the class.
Peter sat at the back of the class.

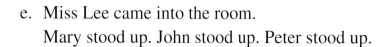

e. Miss Lee came into the room.
Mary stood up. John stood up. Peter stood up.

f. Miss Lee said, "Please sit down."
Mary sat down. John sat down. Peter sat down.

g. Miss Lee wrote on the board.
The children wrote in their books.

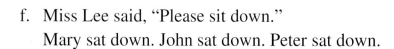

16

h. At ten o'clock they went to the playground.

i. Mary ate an apple.
John ate a cookie.
Peter ate an orange.

j. At a quarter after ten they went back
into the classroom.
Miss Hall came in.
They all stood up. Then they sat down.

k. The children drew on the board.
Mary drew a fish.
John drew a cat.
Peter drew a ball.

l. At one o'clock they went home.

m. Mary saw a man with some balloons.
"Look!" she said to the boys.
Then the boys saw the balloons.

n. Mary bought a red balloon.
John bought a blue balloon.
Peter did not buy a balloon.
He did not have any money.

17

3. *These questions are about page 16 and page 17.*
   Read the questions. Give the answers.

    a. Did Mary go to school by car?
        No, she did not go to school by car.
        She went to school by bus.

    b. Did John wear blue pants?
    c. Did Peter go to school at nine o'clock?
    d. Did Mary sit in the front of the class?
    e. Miss Lee came into the room. Did John sit down?
    f. Miss Lee said, "Please sit down." Did Peter stand up?
    g. Did Miss Lee write in Mary's book?
    h. Did Mary go to the playground at ten-thirty?
    i. Did Peter eat an apple?
    j. Did John go back to the classroom at ten o'clock?
    k. Did Mary draw a cat on the board?
    l. Did Peter go home at twelve-thirty?
    m. Did Mary see a woman with some balloons?
    n. Did John buy a red balloon?

4. *Give short answers to these questions about page 16.*

    a. Did John go to school by car?   Yes, he did.
    b. Did Mary go to school by car?   No, she did not.
    c. Did John wear a green shirt?
    d. Did Mary wear a blue dress?
    e. Did the children get to school at seven-thirty?
    f. Did Mary sit at the back of the class?
    g. Did Peter sit at the back of the class?
    h. Did the children write in their books?

5. *Give answers like these.*

    a. Did you have apples for breakfast this morning?
       No, I did not. I had eggs.
    b. Did you come to school by bus today?
       Yes, I did *or* No, I did not. I came by car.
    c. Did you get to school at seven o'clock this morning?
    d. Did you sit at the back of the class yesterday?
    e. Did you sit at the front of the class yesterday?
    f. Did you write on the board yesterday?
    g. Did you go into the playground yesterday?
    h. Did you eat an apple last night?
    i. Did you see a cat in your desk yesterday?
    j. Did you take a walk this afternoon?

6. *Finish these sentences.*

    a. Yesterday I wore . . .   f. Last night I saw . . .
    b. Last night I ate . . .   g. Yesterday I took . . .
    c. Last week I bought . . .   h. Last year I had . . .
    d. Yesterday I went . . .   i. Last week I wrote . . .
    e. This morning I came . . .   j. Yesterday the teacher drew . . .

7. *Learn these.*

go—went	wear—wore	get—got	buy—bought
come—came	stand—stood	say—said	sit—sat
eat—ate	draw—drew	see—saw	take—took
			write—wrote

8. *Read aloud.*

-ed	= t	walked	looked	knocked	thanked
-ed	= d	smiled	opened	closed	cleaned
-ed	= id	pointed			

1. *Read and answer the questions.*

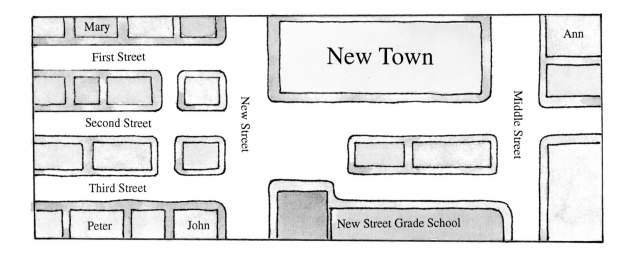

Ann, Mary, Peter, and John live in New Town.

Mary lives on First Street.
Peter and John live on Third Street.
Ann lives on Middle Street.

They all go to New Street Grade School.

Mary goes to school by bus.
Ann does not go to school by bus. She goes by car.
Peter and John do not go to school by bus. They walk to school.

The children do not go to school every day.
They do not go to school on Saturdays and Sundays.

Where do you live?
Do you go to school by bus?
Do you go to school on Sundays?

2. *Read and answer the questions.*

a. Every morning Peter wakes up at seven o'clock.
b. He gets out of bed.
c. His brother wakes up and gets out of bed, too.
d. They wash their faces.
e. They brush their teeth.
f. They put on their clothes.
g. They comb their hair.
h. They eat their breakfast.
i. They say good-bye to their mother and they go to school.

What do you do every morning?
What does your father do every morning?
What do your friends do every morning?

3. *Give short answers to these questions about page 20.*

    a. Does Ann live in New Town?   Yes, she does.

    b. Does Mary live in Old Town?   No, she does not.

    c. Do all the children live in New Town?   Yes, they do.

    d. Do some of the children live in Old Town?   No, they do not.

    e. Does Mary live on First Street?

    f. Does Peter live on First Street?

    g. Do all the children live on Middle Street?

    h. Do all the children go to New Town Grade School?

    i. Does Mary go to school by bus?

    j. Does Ann go to school by bus?

    k. Do Peter and John go to school by bus?

    l. Do Peter and John walk to school?

    m. Do the children go to school every day?

    n. Do the children go to school on Mondays?

    o. Do the children go to school on Sundays?

4. *Give short answers to these questions about page 21.*

    a. Does Peter wake up at seven o'clock?

    b. Does he stay in bed?

    c. Does his brother wake up and get out of bed, too?

    d. Do they wash their faces and brush their teeth?

    e. Do they put on their clothes and comb their hair?

    f. Do they eat their dinner then?

    g. Do they go to a shop then?

    h. Do they go to school?

5. *Answer* Yes, I do, No, he does not, Yes, we do, *etc.*

    a. Do you live in Old Town?

    b. Do you sing songs at school?

    c. Do you learn English at school?

    d. Does your teacher wear a hat?

    e. Do the girls play baseball in the playground?

    f. Do the boys play baseball in the playground?

6. *Read.*

a.

A baby is a small child.
  It cries.

b.

A firefighter is a brave man.
  He puts out fires.

c.

A thief is a bad person.
  He steals things.

d.

A fool is a foolish person.
  He says foolish things.

e.

Soldiers are brave men.
  They fight.

f.

Laborers are strong men.
  They work hard.

g.

Teachers are clever men and women.
  They teach in schools.

23

7. *Answer these questions. The answers are on page 23.*

a. What does a baby do?
   It cries.

b. What does a firefighter do?

c. What does a thief do?

d. What does a fool do?

e. What do soldiers do?
   They fight.

f. What do laborers do?

g. What do teachers do?

8. *Read.*

a. A doctor works in a hospital.

b. Nurses help doctors.

c. A storekeeper looks after a store.

d. A gardener looks after a garden.

e. A maid looks after a home.

f. A bus driver drives a bus.

g. Fishermen catch fish.

h. Farmers work on a farm.

i. Sailors work on a ship.

j. An office worker works in an office.

9. *Ask and answer questions like these about the people on page 24.*

A: What does a doctor do?   A: What do nurses do?
B: He works in a hospital.   B: They help doctors.

10. Review.

a. *Use this table to make sentences like these.*

He is hungry. He is having dinner.
They are happy. They are having a party.

| He is
She is
They are | tired.
hungry.
happy.
hot.
dirty. | He is
She is
They are | having | a party.
a meal.
dinner.
a drink. |
| | | | taking | a nap.
a bath.
a ride. |

b. *Answer the questions.*

1. Did you go to school yesterday?
   Yes, I did. I went to school.
   or No, I did not. I did not go to school.
2. Did you go to school by bus yesterday?
3. Did you walk to school yesterday?
4. Did you clean the board yesterday?
5. Did you write in your book yesterday?
6. Did you see an airplane yesterday?
7. Did you look at the board yesterday?
8. Did you eat something yesterday?

11. *Read aloud.*

-ew   new   draw-drew   blow-blew

25

1. *Read.*

a.

John is holding a bat.

He is going to hit the ball.

b.

Mary is turning on the faucet.

She is going to wash the dishes.

c.

Mrs. Hall is looking at the fruit.

She is going to buy some oranges.

d.

Mrs. Hall is opening her purse.

She is going to pay the man.

e.

The men are digging.

Look at the earth.

They are going to build a big building.

f.

Peter is naughty.

He is hiding behind the bush.

He is going to frighten the children.

g.

Ann is holding a ruler.

She is going to measure the board.

h.

The snake is dangerous.

The children are going to run away.

i.

The building is dangerous.

It is not safe.

It is going to fall down.

j.

The package is falling out of Mrs. Lee's bag.

She is going to lose it.

k.

Mrs. Hall is carrying a basket of clothes.

She is going to wash the clothes.

l.

Ann is looking at the dress in the window.

She is going to buy the dress.

2. *Ask and answer questions like these about the people on page 26 and page 27.*

A: What is John going to do?
B: He is going to hit the ball.

A: What is Mary going to do?
B: She is going to wash the dishes.

3. *Read.*

a.

I am hungry. Eat the cookie, John.

b. I am thirsty. Drink some water, Mary.

c. I am cold. Put on your coat, Peter.

d. I am hot. Take off your coat, Ann.

e. I am tired. Take a nap, Tom.

f. I am brave. Jump into the water, John.

g. I am a firefighter. Please put out the fire.

4. *Ask and answer questions like these about the people on page 28.*

A: What is John going to do?
B: He is going to eat the cookie.

A: What is Mary going to do?
B: She is going to drink some water.

5. *Answer the questions.*

a. What are you going to do at the end of this lesson?
b. What are you going to do tonight?
c. What are you going to do tomorrow?
d. What are you going to do next Saturday?
e. What are you going to do next Sunday?

6. *Read aloud.*

-t   it   sit   get   fat   hat   hot   lot   not   eat   foot   want

blanket   bucket

-te   gate   kite   plate   white

write

bite   ate

-st   fast   breakfast   -ft   left   lift

29

7. Review.

	Every day	Yesterday	Today	Tomorrow
a.	cleans	cleaned	cleaning	going to clean
b.	cooks	cooked	cooking	going to cook
c.	draw	drew	drawing	going to draw
d.	buys	bought	buying	going to buy
e.	wear	wore	wearing	going to wear

Make sentences like these.

a. Every day Mrs. Hall cleans something.
   Yesterday she cleaned the window.
   Today she is cleaning the wall.
   Tomorrow she is going to clean the door.
b. Every day Mrs. Lee cooks something.
   Yesterday she cooked some rice.
c. Every day the children draw something.
d. Every day Mrs. Hall buys something.
e. Every day the boys wear shirts.

30

8. *How many true sentences can you make?*

a.

Our teacher Ice Fire A baby A soldier The sea A flower	is	very	hot. clever. deep. small. cold. brave. beautiful.

b.

I	like do not like	dogs. cookies. snakes. holidays. cars. flowers. flies.	They are very	nice. dangerous. dirty. noisy. beautiful. ugly. useful.

9. *Read aloud.*

-ld	old	hold	cold	child	build
-lk	walk	chalk	talk	milk	
-lf	half				
-lp	help				

The indirect object

1. *Read.*

a.

What is the woman giving John?

She is giving him a candy.

b.

What is Mary showing Peter?

She is showing him a flower.

c.

What is the teacher reading the children?

She is reading them a story.

d.

What is the storekeeper selling Mr. Bell?

He is selling him a newspaper.

e.

What is Mrs. Bell cooking for the children?

She is cooking them a fish.

f.

What is Mrs. Lee buying for the children?

She is buying them ice cream.

g.

What is John giving Peter?

He is giving him his ruler.

h.

What is Mrs. Lee making Tom?

She is making him some pants.

i.

What is the woman sending John and Mary?

She is sending them a package.

j.

What is the mail carrier bringing the children?

He is bringing them a package.

2. *Look at the pictures and answer the questions.*

   a. What did the woman give John?
      She gave him a candy.

   b. What did Mary show Peter?

   c. What did the teacher read the children?

   d. What did the storekeeper sell Mr. Bell?

   e. What did Mrs. Bell cook for the children?

   f. What did Mrs. Lee buy for the children?

   g. What did John give Peter?

   h. What did Mrs. Lee make Tom?

   i. What did the woman send John and Mary?

   j. What did the mail carrier bring the children?

1. *Read.*

a.

Is the airplane moving quickly or slowly?

It is moving quickly.

b.

Is the girl walking quietly or noisily?

She is walking quietly.

c.

May I have some ice cream, please? Thank you.

Is the girl speaking politely or rudely?

She is speaking politely.

d.

Is the man shouting loudly or whispering softly?

He is shouting loudly.

e.

Is the boy writing well or badly?

He is writing badly.

f.

Is the car moving backwards or forwards?

It is moving backwards.

g.

What did John do yesterday?

He played baseball.

h.

What is Mary going to do tomorrow?

She is going to go to school.

i.

What did Tom and Peter do last Saturday?

They went to the movies.

j.

What are the girls going to do next Saturday?

They are going to swim in the sea.

k.

What is Mimi going to do tonight?

She is going to do her homework.

2. *Answer the questions.*

   a. What did you do yesterday?
   b. What are you going to do tomorrow?
   c. What did you do last Saturday?
   d. What are you going to do next Saturday?
   e. What are you going to do tonight?

3. *Read.*

a. Mary wakes up at seven o'clock every morning.

b. She has her breakfast at seven-thirty every morning.

c. She goes to school at eight o'clock every morning.

d. She has her first lesson at a quarter after eight every morning.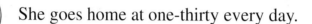

e. She goes home at one-thirty every day.

f. She has lunch at two o'clock every day.

g. She does her homework at six o'clock every day.

h. She has dinner at seven o'clock every night.

i. She goes to bed at ten o'clock every night.

j. What do you do every day?

4. *Read aloud.*

-nd	end	bend	friend	blind	behind	hand
	round		playground		second	

-nt	cent	count	front	point	paint

36

5. *Make one sentence about each picture like this.*

a. She is dancing happily.

b. He is crossing the street carefully.

a.

She is dancing. She is happy.

b.

He is crossing the street. He is careful.

c.

He is walking. He is slow.

d.

He is writing. He is careless.

e.

They are playing. They are noisy.

f.

He is pushing. He is rude.

g.

He is shutting the door. He is quiet.

6. *Answer these questions about Mary. The answers are on page 36.*

a. What time does Mary wake up?
   She wakes up at seven o'clock every morning.

b. What time did she wake up yesterday?
   She woke up at seven o'clock.

c. What time does Mary have breakfast?

d. What time did she have breakfast yesterday?

e. What time does she go to school?

f. What time did she go to school yesterday?

g. What time does she have her first lesson?

h. What time did she have her first lesson yesterday?

i. What time does she go home?

j. What time did she go home yesterday?

k. What time does she do her homework?

l. What time did she do her homework yesterday?

m. What time does she go to bed?

n. What time did she go to bed yesterday?

7. Review. *Change the sentences like this.*

Mrs. Bell gave a candy to John.
She gave him a candy.

Mrs. Lee bought ice cream for the children.
She bought them ice cream.

a. Mary showed a flower to Peter.

b. Mrs. Lee made some pants for Tom.

c. Miss Rose read a story to the children.

d. The shopkeeper sold a newspaper to Mr. Bell.

e. Mrs. Bell cooked some fish for the children.

f. John gave his ruler to Peter.

g. The woman sent a package to John and Mary.

h. The mail carrier brought a present for the children.

1. *Make true sentences.*

a.

In the morning I	always usually often sometimes never	see	a bus. a horse. a train. an airplane. a car.

b.

A bookstore	always usually often sometimes never	sells	meat. writing paper. books. newspapers. schoolbooks.

c.

We	always usually often sometimes never	find	sand bottles rocks pieces of paper money	by the sea.

d.

In the evening I	always usually often sometimes never	eat	rice. fish. meat. bread. flowers.

e.

On Saturdays I	always usually often sometimes never	ride	on a bicycle. on a train. on a bus. in a car. in an airplane.

2. *Read and answer these questions.*

Do you ever ride on a bicycle?

Which answer is true?

Yes, I sometimes/often ride on a bicycle.

No, I never ride on a bicycle.

3. *Answer these questions.*

   a. Do you ever ride on a bicycle?

   b. Do you ever ride on a bus?

   c. Do you ever ride on a train?

   d. Do you ever ride in an airplane?

   e. Do you ever ride in a car?

   f. Do you ever wash your face?

   g. Do you ever brush your teeth?

   h. Do you ever polish your shoes?

4. *Ask your friends questions. Use* ever. *Use these words:*

play baseball, swim in the sea, swim in a river, go to the movies,
ride on a horse, read a book, write a letter, go to a shop,
write with a pencil.

A: Do you ever play baseball?
B: Yes, I often play baseball.

5. *Now answer these questions.*

    a. Does your father ever drive a car?
        No, he never drives a car.
        Yes, he sometimes drives a car.
    b. Does your mother ever drive a car?
    c. Does your mother ever go to the market?
    d. Does your father ever go to the market?
    e. Does your teacher ever read you a story?
    f. Does your teacher ever draw on the board?
    g. Do your friends ever play with you?
    h. Do your father and mother ever take you for a walk?
    i. Do you ever lose your ruler?
    j. Do you ever find a book on the floor?

6. *Finish these sentences.*

    a. In the morning I always . . .
    b. In the morning we often . . .
    c. In the morning I never . . .
    d. In the morning I sometimes . . .
    e. In the morning I usually . . .
    f. In the morning my father always . . .
    g. In the morning my mother always . . .
    h. In the afternoon I sometimes . . .
    i. In the afternoon we always . . .
    j. In the afternoon I never . . .
    k. In the afternoon I sometimes . . .
    l. In the afternoon I usually . . .

    m. In the afternoon I often . . .
    n. In the evening I always . . .
    o. In the evening I sometimes . . .
    p. In the evening I usually . . .
    q. In the evening my father always . . .
    r. In the evening my mother often . . .
    s. In the evening I never . . .
    t. At night I always . . .
    u. At night I never . . .
    v. At night I sometimes . . .
    w. At night my father always . . .
    x. At night my mother always . . .

7. *Read aloud.*

    -oy   **oi**   boy   toy   point   noise   voice

8. *Read.*

a.

John is always early for school.

b.

Peter is sometimes late for school.

c.

Mary is always cheerful.

d.

Ann is sometimes sleepy.

9. *Ask your friend questions like these. He or she can give true answers.*

Are you ever	late for school? early for school? cheerful? sleepy? sad? happy? tired? cold? hot? brave? dirty? hungry? thirsty? careful? careless? noisy? polite? rude? frightened? naughty?	Yes, No,	I am	often sometimes always usually never	late for school. early for school. cheerful. sleepy. sad. happy. tired. cold. hot. brave. dirty. hungry. thirsty. careful. careless. noisy. polite. rude. frightened. naughty.

42

10. *Make sentences like the ones in red.*

a. fall — He often falls down.
    fell — Yes, he fell down yesterday.

b. wake — She sometimes wakes up at eight o'clock.
    woke — Yes, she woke up at eight o'clock yesterday.

c. hide — The dog always hides behind the door.
    hid — Yes, it . . .

d. give — He usually gives him ice cream.
    gave — Yes, . . .

e. sell — He sometimes sells him a newspaper.
    sold

f. know — He always knows the answers.
    knew

g. dig — They often dig a hole.
    dug

h. send — He sometimes sends her a package.
    sent

i. leave — She always leaves home at eight o'clock.
    left

j. ring — The teacher sometimes rings a bell.
    rang

11. *Read aloud.*

-igh   high   light   right   fight   tight   frighten

43

Which?

1. *Read and answer the questions.*

a. Which one is bigger than the others? No. 1.
b. Which one is smaller than the others?
c. Which ones are the same?
d. Which ones are round?
e. Which one is square?

Where?

2. *Read the questions and answers.*

a.

Where is the red book?
It is between the blue books.

b.

Where is the blue book?
It is under the red book.
Where is the green book?
It is on top of the red book.

c.

Where is your wrist?
It is between my hand and my arm.

d.

Where is your chin?
It is below my mouth.
Where is your nose?
It is above my mouth.

e.

Where is the dog running?
It is running across the street.

f.

Where did the ball go?
It went through the window.

g.

Where did the ball fall?
It fell into the bowl of soup.

h.

Where does a fish live?
It lives in the water.

When?

3. *Answer the questions.*

a. When do you wake up?
b. When did you get to school this morning?
c. When did school start this morning?
d. When are you going to have dinner?
e. When are you going home?
f. When does your father get home from work?

What?

4. *Read the questions and answers.*

a.

What is the girl doing?

She is jumping rope.

b.

What is the girl doing?

She is kneeling.

c.

What is the woman doing?

She is shaking the doormat.

d.

What is the woman doing?

She is pouring tea into the cup.

5. *Read aloud.*

| -mp |  jump |  lamp |  stamp |

46

6. *Read.*

a.

What is the dog doing?

It is running away.

What is the man doing?

He is running after it.

b.

What is the woman doing?

She is sewing.

She is fixing the pants.

Whose?

Ann

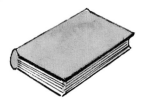

John

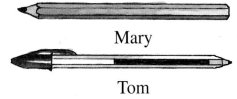

Mary

Tom

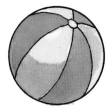

Peter

Bob

Miss Lee

7. *Read aloud.*

a. Whose book is it?   It is John's.
b. Whose ruler is it?   It is Ann's.
c. Whose pencil is it?   It is Mary's.
d. Whose ball is it?   It is Peter's.
e. Whose shirt is it?   It is Bob's.
f. Whose pen is it?   It is Tom's.
g. Whose car is it?   It is Miss Lee's.

8. a. *Answer these questions.*

1. What is your name?
2. Where do you live?
3. Where is your school?
4. When is your birthday?
5. Where do you go on Saturdays?
6. Where did you go last Sunday?
7. Whose pen are you holding?
8. Which teacher teaches you English?

b. *Finish these questions.*

1. What is he doing?
   He is writing in his book.
2. _____ does she live?
   She lives in New Town.
3. _____ is his name?
   His name is Tom.
4. _____ does he go to bed?
   He goes to bed at nine o'clock.
5. _____ book is it?
   It is John's book.

9. *Read aloud.*

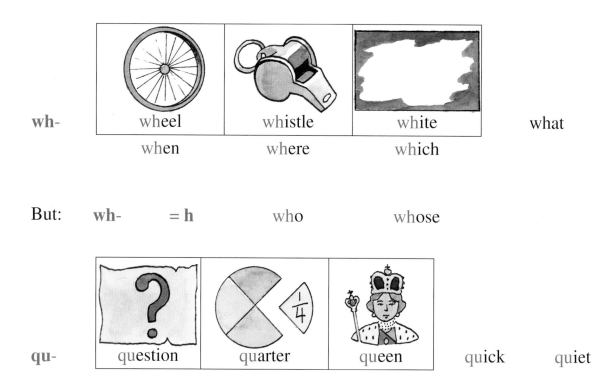

wh-	wheel	whistle	white	what
	when	where	which	

But: **wh-**   **= h**   who   whose

qu-	question	quarter	queen	quick	quiet

48

10. Review. *Answer the questions.*

    a. Do you go to school quickly or slowly?

    b. Do you go home from school quickly or slowly?

    c. Do you walk into your classroom quietly or noisily?

    d. Do you speak to your teacher rudely or politely?

    e. Do you write well or badly?

    f. What did you do yesterday?

    g. What are you going to do tomorrow?

    h. What are you going to do next Sunday?

    i. What did you do last Saturday?

    j. What time do you have breakfast every morning?

    k. What time do you wake up every morning?

    l. What time do you go to bed every evening?

    m. Do you write carefully or carelessly?

    n. Do you cross the street carefully or carelessly?

    o. Does your teacher write quickly or slowly?

    p. Do buses usually move forwards or backwards?

    q. Do bookstores usually sell books or meat?

    r. Do bookstores ever sell newspapers?

11. Review. *How many questions can you make? Answer them.*

Does	your father your mother your teacher your friend	ever	play baseball? draw pictures? swim in the sea? ride on a train? ride on a bicycle? do homework? sing songs? drive a bus?
Do	your father and mother your friends dogs you		

1. *Read.*

a.

The teacher is talking to the children.
Who is she talking to?
She is talking to the children.
Who are the children listening to?
They are listening to the teacher.

b.

What are they waiting for?

They are waiting for a bus.

c.

What is the woman looking for?

She is looking for her glasses.

d.

What is the little boy playing with?

He is playing with his top.

e.

Who is the boy hiding from?

He is hiding from his father.

2. *Read.*

The man is running after the dog.
The man is shouting at the dog.
The police officer is pointing at the dog.
The woman is looking at the dog.
The girl is smiling at the dog.
The boy is laughing at the dog.

Make five sentences like this one. Then answer them.

What is the man running after?

3. *Answer these questions.*

    a. What do you write with?
    b. What do you draw with?
    c. What do you point with?
    d. What do you talk with?
    e. What do you measure with?
    f. What do you eat with?

4. *Now make some more questions using* with.

Here are some words: walk/legs; see/eyes; hear/ears;
hold things/hands; touch things/fingers.

A: What do we walk with?
B: We walk with our legs.

5. Review. *Finish the questions about the picture on the next page.*
Add What, Which, Where, When, *or* Whose.

a. . . . are the children going?
b. . . . are they carrying?
c. . . . is the teacher standing?
d. . . . is the teacher looking at?
e. . . . time is it?
f. . . . does school begin?
g. . . . boy is tall?
h. . . . boy is short?
i. . . . girl is tall?
j. . . . girl is short?
k. . . . are the children carrying?
l. . . . bag is blue?
m. . . . bag is green?
n. . . . bag is red?

Now complete these in the same way.

a. . . . bag is yellow?
b. . . . are the boys doing?
c. . . . are the girls doing?
d. . . . bag is smaller than the others?
e. . . . bag is bigger than the others?
f. . . . is the police officer pointing at?
g. . . . is the dog running after?
h. . . . is the dog running?
i. . . . is the blue car?
j. . . . is the yellow car?
k. . . . are the people at the bus stop waiting for?
l. . . . window in the school is round?
m. . . . window in the school is square?
n. . . . is the police officer holding up?

1. *Answer the questions.*

John Peter Mr. Bell Mr. Lee Mrs. Hall Mrs. Lee

a. Who is the boy with the ball?
    The boy with the ball is John.
b. Who is the boy with the airplane?
c. Who is the man with glasses?
d. Who is the man with the yellow hat?
e. Who is the woman with a basket?
f. Who is the woman with an umbrella?

$50 $60 $40 $90 $10

g. How much is the dress with the yellow collar?
    The dress with the yellow collar is fifty dollars.
h. How much is the dress with red flowers?
i. How much is the dress with green polka dots?
j. How much is the coat with blue buttons?
k. How much is the bag with the yellow handle?

2. *Answer the questions. Use these words:*

holding a fishnet, fishing, listening to the radio, kneeling, running after the dog, swimming, sleeping, throwing a ball, catching a ball.

a. What is the woman on the rock doing?
   The woman on the rock is listening to the radio.
b. What is the man on the rock doing?
c. What is the man in the boat doing?
d. What is the girl in the boat doing?
e. What is the boy in the water doing?
f. What is the boy on the sand doing?
g. What is the woman on the sand doing?
h. What is the girl on the sand doing?
i. What is the girl in the water doing?

3. *Read aloud.*

Silent letters

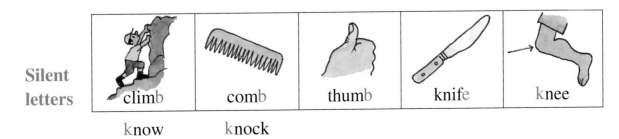

| climb | comb | thumb | knife | knee |

know   knock

55

4. Review. *Ask and answer the questions about the picture.*

| Which | man

woman

boy

girl | is | sitting on the bench?
standing behind the bench?
carrying a basket?
looking in the shop window?
holding the kite?
playing with a top?
holding a doll?
opening a basket? | The one | with the white hat.
in the yellow shirt.

behind the bus.
in the yellow dress.

with the red shirt.
under the tree.
with long hair.
on the grass. |

5. *Some new words and some old ones.*

a.

The building is burning.

The firefighter is not afraid.

He is brave.

He is fighting the fire bravely.

b.

The man is foolish.

He is walking foolishly.

The children are laughing.

The man is very funny.

c.

The knife is sharp.

It can cut easily.

The boy is holding the knife carefully.

He is not holding it dangerously.

d.

The writing is very neat.

Mary is writing neatly.

John's work is not neat.

It is very messy.

e.

Mary's clothes are neat.

John's clothes are messy.

The weather

1. *Read.*

a.

It is cold today.

b.

It is cool today.

c.

It is warm today.

d.

It is hot today.

e.

It is wet today.

It is raining.

f.

It is dry today.

It is not raining.

2. *Answer the questions.*

How is the weather today? How was the weather yesterday?

Today	it	is	hot cold warm cool	and	wet.
Yesterday		was			dry.

Is it raining today?   Yes, it is.   It is wet today.

No, it is not raining today.   It is dry.

Which answer is true?

The four seasons

3. *Read.*

| spring | summer | fall | winter |

a. In **spring** it is cool but it is sunny. This is a good time for walking in the country. We often have picnics.

b. In **summer** it is very hot. We often go to the beach and swim in the sea. Sometimes we have heavy rain. Sometimes it rains heavily and there is a strong wind. This is a storm.

c. In **fall** it is warm but cold weather is coming. The leaves fall off the trees.

d. In **winter** it is cold. Many trees have no leaves. We wear warm clothes. Sometimes it snows.

Numbers

4. *How high can you count? Can you spell the words?*

1	one	19	nineteen
2	two	20	twenty
3	three	21	twenty-one
4	four	22	twenty-two
5	five	30	thirty
6	six	31	thirty-one
7	seven	40	forty
8	eight	50	fifty
9	nine	60	sixty
10	ten	70	seventy
11	eleven	80	eighty
12	twelve	90	ninety
13	thirteen	100	one hundred
14	fourteen	101	a hundred and one
15	fifteen	199	a hundred and ninety-nine
16	sixteen	1,000	one thousand
17	seventeen	10,000	ten thousand
18	eighteen	5,925	five thousand nine hundred and twenty-five

How many?

5. *Read.*

one minute = sixty seconds
There are sixty seconds in one minute.
There are sixty minutes in one hour.
There are twenty-four hours in one day.
There are seven days in one week.
There are four weeks in one month.
There are twelve months in one year.

S	M	T	W	Th	F	S
					1	2
3	4	5	6	7	8	9
10	11	12	13	14	15	16
17	18	19	20	21	22	23
24	25	26	27	28	29	30
31						

6. *Learn this rhyme.*

Thirty days in September,
April, June, and November.
All the rest have thirty-one,
Excepting February alone.
This has twenty-eight days clear.
And twenty-nine in each leap year.

7. *Can you spell these words?*

1	January	7	July
2	February	8	August
3	March	9	September
4	April	10	October
5	May	11	November
6	June	12	December

8. *Can you spell these words?*

1st	first	6th	sixth	11th	eleventh	16th	sixteenth
2nd	second	7th	seventh	12th	twelfth	17th	seventeenth
3rd	third	8th	eighth	13th	thirteenth	18th	eighteenth
4th	fourth	9th	ninth	14th	fourteenth	19th	nineteenth
5th	fifth	10th	tenth	15th	fifteenth	20th	twentieth
						21st	twenty-first

9. *Can you answer these questions?*

January is the first month. Which is the second month?
Which is the third month? Which is the tenth month?
Which is the last month? What is the date today?

60

10. a. *Answer these questions.*

1. What is the weather like today?
2. What was the weather like yesterday?
3. Is it raining today?
4. Was it raining yesterday?
5. Was it raining last Saturday?
6. What is the weather like in winter? In winter it is . . .
7. What is the weather like in spring?
8. What is the weather like in fall?
9. What is the weather like in summer?

b. *Finish these sentences.*

1. January is the first month. It has thirty-one days.
2. February is the _____ month. It has _____ days.
3. March is the _____ month. It has _____ days.
4. April is the _____ month. It has _____ days.
5. May is the _____ month. It has _____ days.
6. June is the _____ month. It has _____ days.
7. July is the _____ month. It has _____ days.
8. August is the _____ month. It has _____ days.
9. September is the _____ month. It has _____ days.
10. October is the _____ month. It has _____ days.
11. November is the _____ month. It has _____ days.
12. December is the _____ month. It has _____ days.

11. *Answer these questions.*

a. How many seconds are there in one minute?
   There are sixty seconds in one minute.
b. How many minutes are there in one hour?
c. How many seconds are there in two minutes?
d. How many minutes are there in two hours?
e. How many hours are there in one day?
f. How many hours are there in two days?

12. *Do you know these words? Some are old but some are new.*

Sometimes	Yesterday
1. I climb a tree.	I climbed a tree.
2. She cooks a meal.	She cooked a meal.
3. She helps her mother.	She helped her mother.
4. He paints a picture.	He painted a picture.
5. We play baseball.	We played baseball.
6. They shout.	They shouted.
7. I talk in class.	I talked in class.
8. We wait for them.	We waited for them.
9. He answers in class.	He answered in class.
10. She looks at the children.	She looked at the children.
11. He washes his car.	He washed his car.
12. The dog jumps over the wall.	The dog jumped over the wall.
13. She walks to school.	She walked to school.
14. He counts the books.	He counted the books.
15. She cleans the windows.	She cleaned the windows.
16. The children clap their hands.	The children clapped their hands.
17. The little girls cry.	The little girls cried.
18. Mrs. Lee carries a basket.	Mrs. Lee carried a basket.
19. We work hard.	We worked hard.
20. We copy from the board.	We copied from the board.
21. He hides behind the door.	He hid behind the door.
22. The dog bites the postman.	The dog bit the postman.
23. The bird flies away.	The bird flew away.
24. We draw on the board.	We drew on the board.
25. The wind blows.	The wind blew.
26. He says, "Hello!"	He said, "Hello!"
27. He brings a kite to school.	He brought a kite to school.
28. She buys some candy.	She bought some candy.
29. He catches the ball.	He caught the ball.
30. Mr. Lee teaches us.	Mr. Lee taught us.

Sometimes	Yesterday
31. He shuts the window.	He shut the window.
32. She hits the ball.	She hit the ball.
33. The storm frightens us.	The storm frightened us.
34. She reads us a story.	She read us a story.
35. The principal speaks to us.	The principal spoke to us.
36. She stands on her chair.	She stood on her chair.
37. A thief steals some money.	A thief stole some money.
38. We see an airplane.	We saw an airplane.
39. He comes to school late.	He came to school late.
40. The dog runs away.	The dog ran away.
41. He falls down.	He fell down.
42. The men dig a hole.	The men dug a hole.
43. He drives a big car.	He drove a big car.
44. He takes his book home.	He took his book home.
45. She wears a blue dress.	She wore a blue dress.
46. He has a cold.	He had a cold.
47. They write in their books.	They wrote in their books.
48. She drinks a glass of milk.	She drank a glass of milk.
49. She gives us candy.	She gave us candy.
50. They go to the movies.	They went to the movies.
51. He hears us.	He heard us.
52. The police officer holds up his hand.	The police officer held up his hand.
53. She kneels on the floor.	She knelt on the floor.
54. I know the answer.	I knew the answer.
55. I lose my ruler.	I lost my ruler.
56. He rides a bicycle.	He rode a bicycle.
57. The teacher rings a bell.	The teacher rang a bell.
58. He sells newspapers.	He sold newspapers.
59. She sends him a letter.	She sent him a letter.
60. She sings to us.	She sang to us.

1. *Read.*

2. *How many sentences can you make?*

Will you	open close touch point to clean	the door, the window, the floor, your book, your desk,	please?

3. *Make sentences like these.*

a pen: "Will you give me a pen, please?" "Yes, here you are!"
some books: "Will you give me some books, please?" "Yes, here you are!"

a. pencil
b. a ruler
c. some pens
d. some rulers
e. a piece of chalk

f. some pieces of paper
g. a glass of milk
h. two boxes of matches
i. a cup of tea
j. three cans of paint

4. *Some new words.*

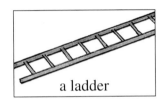
a ladder

a box

Read.

Mr. Bell said, "Children, there is a hole in the roof of our house. I am going to fix it. I am going to work hard! Will you help me, please?"

The children said, "Yes."

Mr. Bell said, "John, will you bring me a ladder, please? Mary, will you bring me a can of red paint, please? Peter, will you bring me a hammer, please? Sam, will you go to the store, please? Will you buy me a box of nails, please? Now I am going to climb up the ladder. John, will you hold the ladder, please? This is hard work, isn't it? I am working hard! I am tired!"

"Yes," said the children. "We are tired, too!"

Answer the questions.

a. Where was the hole?
b. Who brought the ladder?
c. Who brought the can of paint?
d. What color was the paint?
e. Who brought the hammer?

f. Who went to the store?
g. Who bought a box of nails?
h. Who held the ladder?
i. Who was tired?

5. *Two new words:* lend *and* borrow.

John: Will you lend me your ruler, please?
Peter: Yes, here you are.
John: Thank you.
Peter: You're welcome. May I borrow your eraser?
John: Yes, here you are.
Peter: Thank you.
John: You're welcome. May I borrow your pen?
Peter: I'm sorry. I don't have one. Ask Mary.
John: Mary, will you lend me your pen, please?
Mary: Yes, John. Here you are.
John: Thank you.
Mary: You're welcome.

Answer the questions.
a. What did John borrow at first?
b. Who lent John the ruler?
c. What did Peter borrow?
d. Who lent Peter the eraser?
e. What did John borrow next?
f. Who lent John the pen?

6. *Learn the conversation in Exercise No. 5. Practice it around the class. Ask for different things.*

7. *Say these words.*

bag, beg   pan, pen   bad, bed   man, men

8. *Read aloud and spell.*

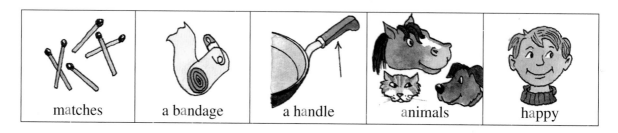

| matches | a bandage | a handle | animals | happy |

The future: will

1. *Read.*

a.

Today I am sick. I am in bed.
　　Tomorrow I will not be in bed.
　　　　Tomorrow I will be better.

b.

Today we are in school.
　　Tomorrow I will not be in school.
　　　　Tomorrow we will be on vacation.

c.

Now Mr. Hall is teaching us.
　　Next class Mr. Hall will not teach us.
　　　　Miss Lee will teach us.

d.

Ann is five today.
　　Next year she will not be five.
　　　　She will be six.

e.

This is a kitten. Next year it will be a cat.
　　Will it be a cat tomorrow?
　　　　No, it won't. It will be a cat next year.

f.

The children are singing now.
　　Will they sing in the next class?
　　　　No, they won't. They will read their books.

g.

"How old are you?"
　　　　　　"I am nine."
"Will you be ten next year?"
　　　　　　"Yes, I will."
"Will you be twelve next year?"
　　　　　　"No, I won't. I will not be
　　　　　　twelve next year. I will be ten."

2. *We write:* I will

We will

He will

She will

It will

They will

You will

We say: I'll

We'll

He'll

She'll

It'll

They'll

You'll

We write: I will not

We will not

He will not

She will not

It will not

They will not

You will not

We say: I won't

We won't

He won't

She won't

It won't

They won't

You won't

3. *Add* not *to these sentences. (The first one is done for you.)*

a. I will do it.
    I will not do it.
b. They will go.
c. She will tell me.
d. He will come tomorrow.

e. They will go home soon.
f. You will see him next week.
g. The store will be closed tomorrow.
h. She will fix his shirt tonight.
i. She will help him tonight.

4. *Change these sentences into questions.*

a. He will be eleven soon.
    Will he be eleven soon?
b. He will go tomorrow.
c. She will see it.

d. I will help her.
e. You will give it to him.
f. It will be cold tomorrow.
g. It will be hot in June.

5. *Read.*

Sammy's Egg

Someone gave Sammy an egg. He was very happy.

"I will not eat it," he thought. "I will keep it. I will keep it in my pocket. It will be warm there. Soon it will become a chicken.

68

The chicken will become a hen. The hen will give me some more eggs. The eggs will become chickens and they will become hens. The hens will give me more eggs. I will sell them. I will be a rich man. I will have many bags of gold. I will live in a big house. The house will have gold doors and windows. It will be very big!"

Then Sammy dropped the egg. "Now I will not be rich," he thought. "I am a silly man." He was sad.

Draw a line under the right words.

a. Someone gave Sammy (one egg, two eggs, many eggs).
b. Then Sammy was very (happy, unhappy, sad).
c. He wanted to become (golden, rich, silly).
d. He (lost, cooked, dropped) the egg.
e. Then he was (rich, poor, sad).

6. *Say these words:* pull, pool   foot, food

7. *Read aloud.*

| a book | a bush | a bookstore | a school | a movie | a pool |

8. **Review.** *Match the sentences under B with the sentences under A.*

A	B
a. Will you turn on the fan, please?	1. I am tired.
b. I am going to take a nap.	2. He is angry.
c. Will you lend me your coat, please?	3. I am hot.
d. The farmer is running after the boy.	4. I am cold.
e. Will you get a doctor, please?	5. She is always cheerful.
f. Will you give me a drink, please?	6. I am sick.
g. She is always smiling.	7. I am sleepy.
h. I am going to bed.	8. I am thirsty.

69

Infinitives of purpose

1.

a. Mary	b. Tom	c. Mrs. Bell	d. Mimi
to see the animals	to get some medicine	to buy some fish	to have a swim
e. Mr. Bell	f. Marigold	g. Martin	h. The children
to get a book	to see her aunt	to buy a kite	to see a movie

Make sentences like these.

a. Mary went to the zoo to see the animals.

b. Tom went to the doctor to get some medicine.

2. *Make five good sentences.*

a.	He turned on the radio		make a dress.	
b.	She bought some cloth		hear some music.	
c.	He went to the store	to	buy some clothes.	
d.	He bought a newspaper		send to her aunt.	
e.	She bought a postcard		read the news.	

3. *Make one sentence about each person. Use* to.

a.

Mrs. Rose is going to the market.

She wants to buy some fish.

Mrs. Rose is going to the market to buy some fish.

b.

John is going to sit in the library.

He wants to read a book.

John is going to sit in the library to read a book.

c.

Tomorrow Mr. and Mrs. Law will go to New York.

They want to have a vacation.

Tomorrow Mr. and Mrs. Law will go to New York to have a vacation.

d.

Peter went to the post office.

He wanted to buy some stamps.

e.

Mary is going to the library.

She wants to borrow a book.

f. Mrs. Lee is putting hot water in the teapot.

She wants to make some tea.

g. Yesterday Peter went to the hospital.

He wanted to see his brother.

h. The laborer is bringing a ladder.

He wants to climb up to the roof.

i. Last week Mrs. Bell went to a dress store.

She wanted to buy a new dress.

j. John is going to get some water.

He wants to give it to his dog.

k. Last week Tom went to the post office.

He wanted to mail a letter.

l. Mary goes to school in the evening.

She wants to learn English.

1. *Look at the pictures and read the sentences. Then cover the sentences and try to say them.*

a. We use a bucket to carry water.

b. We use chalk to write on the blackboard.

c. We use an envelope to send a letter.

d.  We use a hammer to hit nails.

e. We use a needle to sew clothes.

f. We use a purse to carry money.

g.  We use a knife to cut things.

h. We use a cloth to dust things.

i. We use a clock to tell the time.

j. We use a basket to carry things.

k.  We use the sidewalk to walk on.

l. We use notebooks to write in.

m. We use a drum to make a noise.

n.  We use a bus to go to school.

o. We use flour to make bread.

p.  We use a key to open a door.

q.  We use paint to paint with.

r.  We use a playground to play in.

s.  We use a ladder to climb something.

t. 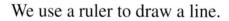 We use a ruler to draw a line.

u.  We use a telephone to talk to people.

v. We use soap and water to wash with.

w.  We use glasses to see with.

x.  We use an eraser to erase things.

y. We use a camera to take pictures.

74

2. *Make sentences like the ones in* red.

    a. Will you give me something to read, please? (a book)
        Yes. Here is a book to read.

    b. Will you give me something to eat, please? (a cracker)
        Yes. Here is a cracker to eat.

    c. Will you give me some money to spend, please? (some money)

    d. Will you give me something to do, please? (some work)

    e. Will you give me something to drink, please? (some tea)

    f. Will you give me something to play with, please? (a ball)

    g. Will you give me something to write with, please? (a pen)

    h. Will you give me something to draw with, please? (a pencil)

    i. Will you give me something to paint with, please? (a brush)

3. *Do the last exercise again but add the words* for you.

    a. Will you give me something to read, please?
        Yes. Here is a book for you to read.

    b. Will you give me something to eat, please?
        Yes. Here is a cracker for you to eat.

4. *Make sentences like the ones in* red.

    a. I have nothing to do. (some work)
        Here is some work for you to do.

    b. My father has nothing to read. (a newspaper)
        Here is a newspaper for your father to read.

    c. My sister has nothing to wear. (a dress)

    d. My cat has nothing to drink. (some milk)

    e. My dog has nothing to eat. (a bone)

    f. My brother has nothing to spend. (some money)

    g. My mother has nothing to cook. (a fish)

    h. John has nothing to carry. (a basket)

5. *Read.*

A Visit to the Zoo

Tomorrow the children are going to the zoo to see the animals. They are going to the monkey house to see the monkeys, and to the lion house to see the lions. Peter and John are going to the snake house to see the snakes. Mary and Ann are going to the bird house.

"John can carry something to eat and Peter can carry something to drink," said Mrs. Lee. "I will give Mary some money to spend."

"I will take some crackers for the monkeys to eat," said Ann.

Answer the questions.

a. Who will see the monkeys?   e. What will John take?
b. Who will see the lions?   f. What will Peter take?
c. Who will see the snakes?   g. What will Mary take?
d. Who will see the birds?   h. What will Ann take?

6. *Say these words.*

kick, cake   tick, take   get, gate   wet, wait   test, taste

7. *Read aloud and spell.*

a face	a plane	a snake	a page	a tablecloth
a nail	rain	a train	a sailor	a straight line

| mail | name | date | brave | dangerous |
| afraid | | great | | gray |

8. **Review.** *Finish these sentences.*

a. Tomorrow I will . . .   d. Tomorrow the children in this class . . .
b. Next year I will . . .   e. Next week we . . .
c. Tomorrow the teacher . . .   f. Soon I . . .

76

Verbs with infinitives

1. *Read.*

Mary likes to listen to the radio.

John likes to watch television.

Mary wants to listen to the radio now.
Mrs. Bell wants her to do her homework.
She is doing her homework.

John wants to watch television now.
Mrs. Bell wants him to polish his shoes.
John is polishing his shoes.

Answer the questions.

a. What does Mary like to do?
b. What does Mary want to do now?
c. What does Mrs. Bell want Mary to do?
d. What does John like to do?
e. What does John want to do now?
f. What does Mrs. Bell want John to do?

2. *Make sentences like the one in red.*

Ann: May I go out?   Ann wants to go out.

a. Ann: May I open the window?
b. Mary: May I close the door?
c. John: May I read my book?
d. Peter: May I sit down?
e. Tom: May I go home?

f. Mimi: May I ask a question?
g. Martin: May I buy an orange?
h. Mary: May I turn on the fan?
i. Ann: May I go to bed?
j. Peter: May I play baseball?

3. *How many sentences can you make?*

Mrs. Lee Mr. Lee Mary	wanted helped	Peter Tom John	to	put the books on the shelf. finish his homework. wash the glasses.

4. *Make sentences like the one in blue.*

Mrs. Lee: Sit down, Mary.
Mrs. Lee told Mary to sit down.

a. Mrs. Lee: Stand up, Mary.
b. The teacher: Sit down, John.
c. The teacher: Stand up, John.
d. Mr. Lee: Sit down, Peter.

e. Mr. Hall: Clean the board, John.
f. Mrs. Lee: Polish your shoes, Peter.
g. Mrs. Lee: Eat your orange, Mary.
h. Miss Lee: Give me your books, children.

5. *Make sentences like the one in red.*

The teacher: Don't talk, children.
The teacher told the children not to talk.

a. Mrs. Lee: Don't shout, children.
b. Miss Lee: Don't run, Mary.
c. Mr. Lee: Don't sing, Peter.
d. Mrs. Lee: Don't laugh, John.

e. Mrs. Lee: Don't be late, children.
f. Miss Lee: Don't look, children.
g. Mr. Chan: Don't be afraid, children.
h. Mrs. Lee: Don't be silly, Peter.

6. *Finish the sentences in red.*

a. John: May I go out, please?   John wants to go . . .
b. Peter: Please help me, Mary.   Peter wants Mary to . . .
c. Mary: I listen to the radio every day.   Mary likes to . . .
d. Mr. Rose: Close the door, Peter.   Mr. Rose told Peter . . .
e. Miss Lee: Don't run, Peter.   Miss Lee told Peter not . . .
f. Miss Best: Don't be afraid, Mary.   Miss Best told Mary . . .
g. Peter watches television every evening.   Peter likes . . .
h. Ann: May I sit down, please?   Ann wants . . .
i. Mr. White: Stand up, John.   Mr. White told . . .
j. Mrs. Bell: Eat your dinner, children.   Mrs. Bell told . . .
k. The teacher: Stop talking, children.   The teacher told . . .
l. Mr. Long: Don't write carelessly, Peter.   Mr. Long told . . .

7. *Read.*

The Baseball Game

Every Saturday Mr. Hall and Mr. Bell like to watch a baseball game. Mr. Hall always remembers to take his umbrella but Mr. Bell sometimes forgets to take his umbrella.

Last Saturday they went to town to watch a baseball game. Mr. Hall remembered to take his umbrella but Mr. Bell forgot to take his umbrella. The game began at three o'clock. It began to rain at three-thirty. Mr. Hall tried to help Mr. Bell. He tried to hold his umbrella over Mr. Bell but Mr. Bell was very wet.

"You must go home," said Mr. Hall.

a. What do Mr. Hall and Mr. Bell like to do?
b. Who always remembers to take his umbrella?
c. Who sometimes forgets to take his umbrella?
d. Where did they go last Saturday?
e. Who remembered to take his umbrella?
f. Who forgot to take his umbrella?
g. When did the game begin?
h. When did it begin to rain?
i. What did Mr. Hall try to do?
j. Who went home?

8. *Read aloud and spell.*

fall	a drawing	tall	a saucer	a dog

9. **Review.** *What do we use these things for?*

a pencil a pen a paintbrush
a hammer chalk a ruler

79

1. *Read and answer the questions.*

a.

Mr. Cook	Mr. Wood	Mr. Green
old	older	oldest

Mr. Cook is old.
Mr. Wood is older.
Mr. Green is the oldest.

b.

Tom	Betty	Tim
young	younger	youngest

Tom is young.
Betty is younger.
Tim is the youngest.

c.

bicycle	car	airplane

Which is the slowest?
Which is the fastest?

d.

kitten	cat	dog

Which is the smallest?
Which is the biggest?

e.

girl	man	boy

Who is the happiest?
Who is the saddest?

f.

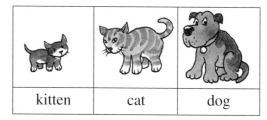

green shirt	yellow shirt	white shirt

Which is the cleanest?
Which is the dirtiest?

g.

$2 + 2$	26×3	$\dfrac{119}{5} \times \dfrac{26}{8}$
Number 1	Number 2	Number 3

Which is the easiest?
Which is the most difficult?

h.

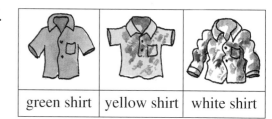

JOHN   PETER   TOM

Who is the most careful?
Who is the most careless?

2. *Read the questions and answer them.*

a. Which streets are wide?
b. Which streets are narrow?

c. Which is the widest of the streets?
d. Which is the narrowest of the streets?

e. Which airplanes are high?
f. Which airplanes are low?

g. Which is the highest of the airplanes?
h. Which is the lowest of the airplanes?

i. Mary's marks are good.
   Whose marks are better?
j. Whose marks are the best?
k. Ann's marks are bad.
   Whose marks are worse?
l. Whose marks are the worst?

3. *Read and answer the questions.*

a. Ann's chair is not very comfortable. Mary's chair is more comfortable than Ann's. Betty's chair is more comfortable than Mary's.
   Whose chair is the most comfortable?

b. Tom's book is more exciting than John's. John's book is more exciting than Peter's.
   Whose book is the most exciting?

4. *Choose the right words.*

a. Marigold was (young, younger, the youngest) girl in the class.
b. Peter is (old, older, the oldest) than his brother.
c. Robert is (bigger, biggest, the biggest) boy in the school.
d. The last exercise was (difficult, more difficult, the most difficult) than the others.
e. The boys' marks were (the worst, worst, worse) than the girls.
f. John's marks were (good, better, the best) in the class.

5. *Read.*

The children wrote some stories for Miss Lee. Miss Lee read them and gave them back to the children.

"Your stories were very good," she said. "Mary's story was the most interesting. I gave her a hundred. John's was the most exciting. I gave him a ninety. Peter's story was the shortest. I gave him a sixty. Ann's was the longest. I gave her a seventy."

a. Whose story was the longest?
b. Whose story was the shortest?
c. Whose story was the most interesting?
d. Whose story was the most exciting?
e. Whose mark was the best?
f. Whose mark was the worst?

6. *Read aloud and spell.*

a.

short	shorter	the shortest
long	old	young
tall	small	cold
brave	thick	strong
weak	cheap	large
clean	clever	narrow
low	wide	

b.

big	bigger	the biggest
fat	hot	sad thin

c.

happy	happier	the happiest
pretty	heavy	dirty
messy	sleepy	ugly
busy	hungry	

d.

beautiful	more beautiful	the most beautiful
careful	careless	difficult
dangerous	exciting	comfortable

7. Review. *Finish the sentences.*

a. I like to . . .
b. I want to . . .
c. My teacher wants me . . .
d. My friend helped me to . . .

e. The teacher told us to . . .
f. My friend asked me to . . .
g. Our teacher told us not . . .
h. Their teacher told them not . . .

UNIT
19   **How much? How old? How often? etc.**

1. *Answer the questions.*

a.

How many boys are there in the swimming pool?
How many girls are there?
How many children are there?
How many steps are there?

b.

How many horses are there?
How many cows are there?
How many sheep are there?
How many animals are there?
How many people are there?

c. How many boys are there in your classroom?
How many girls are there?
How many people are there?

83

2. *Read and answer the questions.*

a.
How much ink is there in the bottle?
The bottle is full.

b.
How much ink is there in the bottle?
The bottle is half full.

c.
How much ink is there in the bottle?
The bottle is empty.
There is no ink.

d.
How much milk is there in the bottle?

e.
How much milk is there in the bottle?

f.
How much chalk is there in the box?

g.
How much chalk is there in the box?

h.
How much rice is there in the bag?

i.
How much tea is there in the cup?

j.
How much paper is there in the cupboard?

84

3. *Learn and practice.*

How much is an orange?

Two fifty.

That is very expensive.
How much are the apples?

Three for one fifty.

That is very cheap.
Please give me five.

That is two fifty, please.

4. *Answer the questions.*

John Bell

122 cm

ten

Mr. Bell

167 cm

thirty-five

Mrs. Bell

162 cm

thirty

Mary Bell

111 cm

eight

a. How old is John Bell?   He is ten years old.
b. How old is Mary Bell?
c. How old is Mrs. Bell's husband?
d. How old is Mr. Bell's wife?
e. How tall is John Bell?   He is 122 centimeters tall.
f. How tall is Mary Bell?
g. How tall is Mrs. Bell's husband?
h. How tall is Mr. Bell's wife?

5. *Read the table. How many questions and answers like these can you make?*

How often do you have English?
We have English once a day.
We have English six times a week.

We have	English mathematics history a meal school music art	once twice three times four times five times six times seven times	a	day. week.

6. *Answer these questions.*

   a. How often do you go to school?
   b. How often does your mother go to the market?
   c. How often do you have homework?
   d. How often do you play with your friends?
   e. How often do you wash your face?
   f. How often do you comb your hair?

7. *Answer these questions.*

   a. How many chairs are there in your classroom?
   b. How many desks are there in your classroom?
   c. How many children are there in your classroom?
   d. How old is your father?
   e. How old is your mother?
   f. How tall is your father?
   g. How tall is your mother?
   h. How much chalk is there in the box on your teacher's desk?
   i. How much water is there in the classroom?

more, fewer, less

1. *Read and answer the questions.*

a.

John	Peter	Mary	Ann	Betty	Tom

Peter has more books than John.
John has fewer books than Peter.
Who has more kittens than Mary?
Who has fewer kittens than Ann?
Who has more apples than Tom?
Who has fewer apples than Betty?

b.

John	Peter	Mary	Ann	Betty	Tom

Peter has more rice than John.
John has less rice than Peter.
Who has more milk than Mary?
Who has less milk than Ann?
Who has more bread than Tom?
Who has less bread than Betty?

2. *How many good sentences can you make?*

John		more	pens		Peter.
Mary			ink		Ann.
The teacher	has	fewer	rulers	than	Betty.
Mr. Bell			paper		Tom.
Miss Lee		less	chalk		Mimi.

87

3. *Make sentences like the ones in blue.*

The man has two dogs. The woman has three dogs.
The woman has more dogs than the man.
The man has fewer dogs than the woman.

John has a little milk. Mary has a lot of milk.
Mary has more milk than John.
John has less milk than Mary.

  a. The boy has two oranges. The girl has three oranges.
  b. The boy has a little water. The girl has a lot of water.
  c. Mrs Lee has three cats. Mrs. Bell has four cats.
  d. Tom has a little money. Mr. Lee has a lot of money.
  e. Ann's book has fifty pages. Tom's book has ninety pages.
  f. The red bottle has a little ink. The blue bottle has a lot of ink.

4. *Put a check ☑ by the best word.*

  a. A library has (more ☐ less ☐ fewer ☐) books than a classroom.
  b. A house has (more ☐ less ☐ fewer ☐) rooms than a school.
  c. A jug can hold (more ☐ less ☐ fewer ☐) milk than a cup.
  d. I have (more ☐ less ☐ fewer ☐) money than my father or mother.
  e. There are (more ☐ less ☐ fewer ☐) days in a year than there are in a month.
  f. There are (more ☐ less ☐ fewer ☐) days in April than there are in March.

5. *Read aloud and spell.*

  o: no   go   ago

o-e: close   those   note   wrote   alone   stone   home   hole

ow: low   know   blow   slow   show   bowl   yellow

oa: boat   coat   road   soap

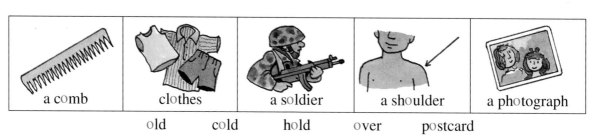

| a comb | clothes | a soldier | a shoulder | a photograph |

old   cold   hold   over   postcard

6. *Read.*

The Clever Son

This is an old story. It was first told long ago. A rich man wanted to make a journey to another town. He was a businessman. He wanted to take things to sell. He also wanted to take gold to buy things with. He decided to take his five sons with him. He wanted his sons to carry the things to sell, and the gold, and also food to eat on the journey.

He was a kind man. He said to one of his sons, "You are the smallest, the thinnest, and the weakest of all my sons. You cannot carry a heavy load. You must choose the lightest load to carry."

The son thanked his father. He pointed to the biggest load. This was bread to eat on the journey.

His father said, "You are foolish. That is the biggest and heaviest load." But the son lifted up the load cheerfully and the journey began. They walked for four hours. Then they stopped for a rest. They all ate some of the bread. Then there was less bread for the son to carry. Every day they ate more bread and there was less bread to carry. The son's load grew smaller and lighter every day. At the end of the journey, the clever son had nothing to carry.

a. Who wanted to go on a journey?
b. What did he want to take?
c. Why did he take gold?
d. Why did he take food?
e. How many sons went?

f. What did he want his sons to do?
g. What did the clever son carry?
h. Why did they stop?
i. What happened to the bread?
j. What happened to the son's load?

7. Review. *Give words with the* opposite *meaning.*

the smallest: the biggest
the youngest
the longest
the cheapest

the slowest
the dirtiest
the saddest
the lowest

the most difficult
the most careful
the narrowest
the best

1. *Finish the sentences.*

a.

John:	$\frac{79}{100}$	well
Mary:	$\frac{85}{100}$	better
Peter:	$\frac{94}{100}$	the best
Ann:	$\frac{14}{100}$	badly
Tom:	$\frac{9}{100}$	worse
Tim:	$\frac{2}{100}$	the worst

John did well in the examination.

Mary did . . .

Peter did . . . of all.

Ann did . . .

Tom did . . .

Tim did . . .

b.

	fast
	faster
	the fastest
	slowly
	more slowly
	the most slowly

A horse moves fast.

A car moves . . .

An airplane moves . . . of all.

A man moves slowly.

A child moves . . .

An old man moves . . .

2. *Read and learn.*

A slow bus moves slowly.	. . . more slowly	. . . the most slowly
A quick boy answers quickly.	. . . more quickly	. . . the most quickly
A loud speaker speaks loudly.	. . . more loudly	. . . the most loudly
A brave soldier fights bravely.	. . . more bravely	. . . the most bravely
A clear writer writes clearly.	. . . more clearly	. . . the most clearly
A fierce lion roars fiercely.	. . . more fiercely	. . . the most fiercely
A neat writer writes neatly.	. . . more neatly	. . . the most neatly
A polite person speaks politely.	. . . more politely	. . . the most politely
A careful writer writes carefully.	. . . more carefully	. . . the most carefully
A careless writer writes carelessly.	. . . more carelessly	. . . the most carelessly
A fast train goes fast.	. . . faster	. . . the fastest
A hard worker works hard.	. . . harder	. . . the hardest
A bad student works badly.	. . . worse	. . . the worst
A good student works well.	. . . better	. . . the best

90

3. *Make sentences like the first one.*

  a. John spoke clearly but Peter spoke more clearly.
  b. He wrote neatly but his sister . . .
  c. A lion can roar fiercely but two lions . . .
  d. She wrote carefully but the other students . . .
  e. Peter moved quickly but Tim . . .
  f. A bicycle can go fast but a car . . .
  g. Betty did well in the test but Ann . . .

4. *Make sentences like the first one.*

  a. All the boys shouted loudly but John shouted the most loudly.
  b. All the soldiers fought bravely but the leader . . .
  c. All the buses go slowly but this bus . . .
  d. They all speak politely but Mary . . .
  e. They all worked hard but Peter . . .
  f. All the men drove dangerously but Tom Bell . . .
  g. All the women spoke softly but Miss Lee . . .

5. *Say these words.*

eat, it	seat, sit	sheep, ship
wheel, will	these, this	reach, rich

6. *Read aloud and spell.*

  e: he   she   me   we   these
  ee: see   three   free   knee   kneel   deep   street
       sweet   sheet   week   asleep   cheerful
  ea: sea   seat   tea   teapot   teacher   leader
       easy   please   speak   meal   steal   leaf
       cheap   cheaply   meat   neat   ice cream
  ie: piece   chief   fierce   fiercely

| a key | people | a police officer | the ceiling |

91

7. *Read.*

The School Chorus

John and Mary were members of the school chorus. Peter and Ann also wanted to be members. They went to see Mr. Lee.

"Please, Mr. Lee," said Peter politely, "we would like to join the chorus."

"Very well," said Mr. Lee, "but you must sing to me first. Here is a song. First I will play it on the piano. Then I want you to sing it carefully."

The children began to sing.

"Stop!" said Mr. Lee. "Peter, you are singing very loudly. Please sing more softly. Ann, you are singing very softly. Please sing more loudly. Go back to the beginning and try again."

Peter sang more softly and Ann sang more loudly.

"Good," said Mr. Lee. "You sang very well. You have clear voices. You sing very clearly. You can join my chorus."

Answer the questions.

a. Was John in the chorus?

b. Was Mary in the chorus?

c. What did Peter and Ann want?

d. Who did they speak to?

e. Who played the piano?

f. Who sang loudly at first?

g. Who sang softly at first?

h. Who had clear voices?

i. Who sang well?

j. Who was pleased?

8. Review. *Answer the questions.*

a. Which has more pages, a book or a chapter?

b. Which has fewer legs, a table or a boy?

c. Which holds more ink, a bottle or a pen?

d. Which holds less water, a cup or a jug?

(not) as . . . as

1. *Read.*

   a. Tim is ten years old. Tom is ten, too, but Alan is twelve.
      Tim is as old as Tom.
      Tim is not as old as Alan.

Tim	Tom	Alan
10 years	10 years	12 years

   b. The bicycle is moving at 25 kilometers per hour.
      The car is also moving at 25 k.p.h. but the airplane is moving at 800 k.p.h.
      The bicycle is moving as fast as the car.
      It is not moving as fast as the airplane.

25 k.p.h.	25 k.p.h.	800 k.p.h.

   c. The red shirt has three buttons. The blue shirt has three buttons too, but the green shirt has four buttons.
      The red shirt has as many buttons as the blue shirt.
      The red shirt does not have as many buttons as the green shirt.

3 buttons	3 buttons	4 buttons

   d. Jane has two glasses of milk. Jill has two glasses of milk too, but Betty has four glasses of milk.
      Jane has as much milk as Jill.
      Jane does not have as much milk as Betty.

Jane	Jill	Betty
2 glasses	2 glasses	4 glasses

2. *How many sentences can you make?*

John	writes		as	quickly	as	Mary.
	does not write			clearly		
				neatly		
The boys	write			carefully		
				carelessly		
	do not write			fast		
				badly		

3. *Make sentences like the ones in red.*

Tim's height is 140 cm. Tom's height is 140 cm. Alan's height is 145 cm. (tall)
Tim is as tall as Tom.
Tim is not as tall as Alan.

  a. Jane's height is 130 cm. Jill's height is 130 cm. Betty's height is 133 cm.
      (tall)
  b. Tim's weight is 35 kg. Tom's weight is 35 kg. Alan's weight is 40 kg.
      (heavy)
  c. First Street is 6 m. wide. Second Street is 6 m. wide. Third Street is 9 m.
      wide. (wide)
  d. Jane's book is 2 cm. thick. Jill's book is 2 cm. thick. Betty's book is 3 cm.
      thick. (thick)

4. *Make sentences like the ones in red.*

John has two pencils. Peter has two pencils. Tom has four pencils.
John has as many pencils as Peter.
John does not have as many pencils as Tom.
Mary has one bottle of ink. Susan has one bottle of ink. Betty has two bottles of
ink.
Mary has as much ink as Susan.
Mary does not have as much ink as Betty.

  a. John has two rulers. Peter has two rulers. Tom has four rulers.
  b. Mary has two cups of tea. Susan has two. Betty has three.
  c. April has thirty days. June has thirty days. March has thirty-one days.
  d. Tim has a loaf of bread. Tom has one too. Alan has three loaves.

5. *Say these words:*   eat, it   heat, hit   leave, live

6. *Read aloud and spell.*

drink	children	ink	kick	different
dinner	easily	engine	English	family
kitten	fisherman	foolishly	history	middle
multiply	lift	listen	little	prisoner
	notice	picture	milk	

7. *Read.*

The Hare and the Tortoise

A hare can run very fast. A tortoise moves very slowly. It carries a heavy shell on its back. It cannot move as quickly as other animals.

One morning a hare said to a tortoise, "I can run faster than you. You are a very slow animal."

"Yes," said the tortoise. "I cannot run as fast as you. But let us have a race. I will race you and I will win. I will run faster than you."

"You are foolish," said the hare, "I will win easily. Let us race to that tree. Are you ready? Go!"

The tortoise began walking slowly towards the tree. He could not go fast. But he did not stop. The hare laughed.

"I will not hurry," he said. "I will lie down to have a little rest. Then I will go after the tortoise and win the race. I can run faster than the tortoise."

The hare lay down and went to sleep. The tortoise moved slowly on. The sun climbed higher into the sky. The tortoise slowly moved nearer the tree but the hare was asleep.

At last the hare woke up. "Now I will run to the tree and win the race," he said. He ran quickly to the tree but the tortoise was there.

"I am slow," said the tortoise, "but I won the race."

a. Which animal runs fast?
b. Which animal moves slowly?
c. What does a tortoise carry?
d. Is the shell heavy?
e. Where did they race?
f. What did the tortoise do?
g. What did the hare do?
h. Which animal moved slowly?
i. Which animal ran quickly?
j. Which animal won?

8. Review. *Answer the questions.*

a. Which goes the fastest, a bicycle, a car, or an airplane?
b. Which runs more quickly, a dog, or a duck?
c. Who speak more loudly, girls, or boys?

1. *Put in* mine, yours, hers, his, ours, *or* theirs.

   a. "Is this my bag or _____?" "It's not my bag. _____ has my name on it.
      It is _____."

   b. "Mary wants to borrow my ruler. She cannot use _____. It is too small.
      I do not want to lend her _____. I want to use it."
      "Ask John to lend her _____. He is not using it."

   c. "Our school is new. Is your school new or old?"
      "_____ is new, too, but it is not as new as _____."

2. *Say what the people in the pictures are doing.*

a. The boys   The boys are having a snack.

b. The Lee family

c. Mary and John

d. Mr. Law

e. John

f. The children

g. Peter

h. The children

i. Mr. Lee

3. *Change the sentences using* Yesterday.

I look at my book.
Yesterday I looked at my book.

I wear a coat.
Yesterday I wore a coat.

1. The mail carrier knocks on the door.
2. Mother opens the package.
3. John walks to school.
4. Mary closes the door.
5. The teacher points to the board.
6. John cleans the board.
7. The teacher thanks John.
8. Mary goes to school by bus.
9. Peter wears a blue shirt.
10. They get to school at eight o'clock.
11. Peter sits at the back of the class.
12. Miss Lee comes to school in a car.
13. The children stand up.
14. The children sit down.
15. Miss Lee writes on the board.
16. Mary eats an apple.
17. The children draw in their books.
18. They see an airplane.
19. John buys some oranges.
20. A woman smiles at us.
21. It is wet.
22. We blow up some balloons.
23. We have fish for dinner.
24. Mrs. Hall cooks some meat.
25. He gives us some candy.
26. The teacher reads to us.
27. He lends me his books.
28. Mrs. Lee makes Tom some pants.
29. He sends us a package.
30. He shows me some pictures.
31. He falls down.
32. She wakes up at seven o'clock.
33. The dog hides behind the door.
34. He sells us pencils and pens.
35. John knows the answer.
36. The laborers dig a hole in the road.
37. Ann leaves home at eight o'clock.
38. The mail carrier rings the bell.
39. It is very cold.
40. It is raining.
41. The boy sees a monkey.
42. We copy from the board.
43. The dog bites the mail carrier.
44. An airplane flies over the school.

4. *Ask questions and answer them.*

A: Look at No. 1. Did you see an airplane yesterday?

B: No, I didn't. I didn't see an airplane yesterday. I saw a bus.

see an airplane?	buy a ruler?	draw a cat?	eat an apple?	wear red shoes?	write a book?	sit on a desk?
a.	b.	c.	d.	e.	f.	g.
a bus	a pen	a dog	an orange	black shoes	a letter	a chair

5. *Make sentences for each row of pictures like these.*

1a. Every day Mrs. Bell cleans something.

1b. Sometimes she cleans a pan.

1c. Yesterday she cleaned the window.

1d. Today she is cleaning the door.

1e. Tomorrow she is going to clean the ceiling.

	Every day	Sometimes	Yesterday	Today	Tomorrow
1. Mrs. Bell	1a. cleans something	1b. cleans a pan	1c. cleaned the window	1d. is cleaning the door	1e. is going to clean the ceiling

| 2. Mrs. Hall | 2a. buys something | 2b. buys some oranges | 2c. bought some apples | 2d. is buying some oranges | 2e. is going to buy a fish |

3. The children

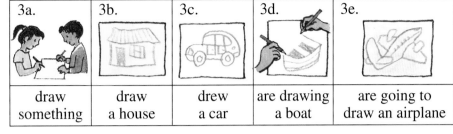

3a.	3b.	3c.	3d.	3e.
draw something	draw a house	drew a car	are drawing a boat	are going to draw an airplane

4. The boys

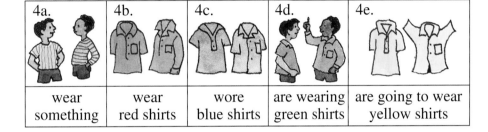

4a.	4b.	4c.	4d.	4e.
wear something	wear red shirts	wore blue shirts	are wearing green shirts	are going to wear yellow shirts

6. *Ask your friend questions like these.*

a. What is your name?
b. What is your father's name?
c. How old are you?
d. How tall are you?
e. Where do you live?
f. Which school do you go to?
g. Where do you sit?
h. What is your teacher doing now?
i. How many books are there on your desk?
j. Whose book are you reading?
k. What do you do on Sundays?
l. What did you do yesterday?
m. What time did you get to school this morning?
n. What is the time now?
o. When are you going to do your homework?
p. How many centimeters are there in a meter?
q. How often do you read a book?
r. What did you see yesterday?
s. What are you going to do tomorrow?
t. How often do you have a birthday?

u. How many people are there in your home?

v. What time do you wake up?

w. How many pages are there in this book?

x. What does a bird do?

y. What does a fish do?

7. *Choose the best answer.*

a. Will you . . . the door, please? (opened, opening, open, opens)

b. The kitten . . . be a cat next year. (are, would, will, is)

c. She went to the cupboard . . . get a book. (to, for, and, too)

d. Here is a biscuit to . . . for breakfast. (eat, ate, eaten, eating)

e. Here is some money . . . you to spend. (to, for, by, from)

f. The teacher told the children . . . a noise. (to not make, not to make, to make not)

g. Mary helped her mother . . . the room. (cleaned, cleaning, cleans, to clean)

h. John likes . . . television. (watch, to watch, watches, watched)

i. Mary helped Ann . . . the homework. (finishing, finished, finishes, to finish)

j. Which of the three girls is . . .? (a prettiest, prettier, the prettiest)

k. A man has . . . legs than a horse. (more, less, fewer)

l. A small jug holds . . . milk than a big one. (more, less, fewer)

m. A car moves . . . than a horse. (fast, faster, more fast, more faster)

n. Tim is not . . . as his brother. (old, older, as old, the oldest)

o. A horse does not move as . . . a car. (fast as, fast than, faster than)

Word List

A
afraid	57
again	92
alone	88
also	89
angry	69
art	86
as	93
aunt	70
away	27

B
back	15
backwards	34
badly	34
bat	26
bath	11
beach	59
because	4
become	68
beg	66
begin	52
beginning	92
below	45
bend	36
between	45
birthday	48
bite	29
blind	36
bone	75
bookstore	39
borrow	66
bravely	57

bring	33
brush	21
build	26
building	26
bush	26
businessman	89

C
camera	74
cent	36
chapter	92
cheap	14
cheerful	42
cheerfully	89
chick	14
chief	91
child	23
chin	14
choose	4
chorus	92
clear	90
clearly	90
cloth	70
cold	13
comb	21
comfortable	81
cool	58
copy	62
count	36
country	59

D
dangerously	57
decide	89
deep	31
difficult	80
dig	26
dish	26
dollars	54
doormat	46
drawing	8
drink	12
drive	24
drop	69
dust	73

E
early	42
earth	26
easily	57
end	29
engine	94
ever	40
every	6
examination	90
exciting	81
expensive	85

F
fall	27
family	11
fewer	87
fierce	90
fiercely	90
find	39

Word List

fishnet	55		homework	35		look after	24
fix	47		husband	85		lose	27
fool	23					loudly	34
foolish	23	**I**	ice	3		low	81
foolishly	57		interesting	82			
forget	79		into	16	**M**	maid	24
forwards	34					map	8
free	91	**J**	join	92		mark	10
frighten	26		journey	89		mathematics	86
funny	57		jump rope	46		meal	11
						measure	27
G game	79	**K**	keep	68		medicine	70
gold	69		kilometer	93		member	92
good-bye	21		know	43		messy	57
got	16					meter	94
grade	20	**L**	ladder	65		monkey	76
great	76		large	82		move	34
grow	89		leader	91		movie	35
			leaf	59		music	70
H half full	84		learn	72			
happen	89		leave	43	**N**	nap	12
happily	37		lend	66		narrow	81
hare	95		less	88		neat	57
heavily	59		lesson	11		neatly	57
height	94		library	71		never	39
hide	26		lift	29		news	70
high	43		light	89		next	29
history	86		lion	76		nice	31
hit	26		live	20		noisily	34
holiday	6		load	89		noisy	31
home	6		loaf	94		notebook	73

Word List

no. (number)	1		
O office	24	**R** race	95
office worker	24	reach	91
often	39	ready	95
once	86	remember	79
other	44	rest	89
		rich	69
P party	12	ride	12
pay	26	roar	90
person	23	rock	39
photograph	88	roof	65
piano	92	rudely	34
place	15		
polish	40	**S** sad	10
politely	34	safe	27
pool	69	say	5
poor	69	seasons	59
postcard	70	seat	91
post office	71	second	60
pour	46	sell	32
present	38	send	33
pretty	100	shake	46
principal	63	sharp	57
prisoner	94	sheep	83
put out	23	sheet	91
		shelf	78
Q quickly	34	shell	95
quietly	34	sick	13
		silly	69
		sleepy	42
		snack	12
		snake	27

snow	59
soap	74
softly	34
sometimes	39
song	22
soon	76
sorry	66
spend	75
stay	22
steal	23
step	83
stockings	3
stop	78
store	24
storekeeper	5
storm	59
straight	76
sunny	59
sweet	91
swimming pool	83
switch	14
T taste	76
teapot	72
television	77
test	76
thank	15
theater	70
thief	23
thirsty	28
through	45

Word List

tick	76	**V** vacation	67	which	44
tight	43	voice	41	whisper	34
times	86			whose	47
tomorrow	29	**W** wake up	21	wide	81
tonight	29	walk	12	wife	85
top	50	warm	58	win	95
tortoise	95	watch	77	worst	81
turn on	26	weather	58	wrist	45
twice	86	week	60		
		weight	94	**Z** zoo	70
U us	2	welcome	66		
useful	31	well	34		
usually	39	when	46		